He Matakite ō Ngā Tangata Māori:
The Māori Oracle

When the first carver, Ruatepupuke, was working on his waka [*canoe*], legend says that it was the Puawerewere [*spiders*] that aided him in his work. It was especially fitting that they left the pattern of the māwhaiwhai [*spiderweb*] behind them as they worked, as it speaks of the manner in which all is connected.

From the ancestral lands of Hawaikī-nui to Aotearoa [*New Zealand*], from past to future, from old to young.

Ki a rātou kua wheturangitia
tīramarama tonu ai i roto i ā mātou ngākau
hai whetu marama, hai whetu arahi

To those who have become as stars,
shine always inside our hearts,
as a bright, guiding star.

My Grateful Thanks...

To Edward and Sophia,
my beloved husband and daughter.

To Cheryl and Bridget,
for their wonderful assistance.

To those Tangata Whenua
who prefer to remain un-named,
for their precious gifts of advice.

To all my friends, whānau,
and to the staff of Schiffer Publishing, Ltd.,
who have supported me and believed.

He whakamihi ki a tatou.

Copyright © 2013 by P.A. Minnell

Library of Congress Control Number: 2012955355

All rights reserved. No part of this work may be reproduced or used in any form or by any means—graphic, electronic, or mechanical, including photocopying or information storage and retrieval systems—without written permission from the publisher.

The scanning, uploading and distribution of this book or any part thereof via the Internet or via any other means without the permission of the publisher is illegal and punishable by law. Please purchase only authorized editions and do not participate in or encourage the electronic piracy of copyrighted materials.

"Schiffer," "Schiffer Publishing, Ltd. & Design," and the "Design of pen and inkwell" are registered trademarks of Schiffer Publishing, Ltd.

Designed by Justin Watkinson   Type set in Rosemary Roman/Book Antiqua

ISBN: 978-0-7643-4384-1
Printed in China
5 4 3 2

Published by Schiffer Publishing, Ltd.
4880 Lower Valley Road
Atglen, PA 19310
Phone: (610) 593-1777; Fax: (610) 593-2002
E-mail: Info@schifferbooks.com

For the largest selection of fine reference books on this and related subjects, please visit our website at **www.schifferbooks.com**. You may also write for a free catalog.

This book may be purchased from the publisher.
Please try your bookstore first.

We are always looking for people to write books on new and related subjects. If you have an idea for a book, please contact us at proposals@schifferbooks.com

Schiffer Books are available at special discounts for bulk purchases for sales promotions or premiums. Special editions, including personalized covers, corporate imprints, and excerpts can be created in large quantities for special needs. For more information contact the publisher.

He Matakite ō Ngā Tangata Māori

THE MĀORI ORACLE

WRITTEN AND ILLUSTRATED BY
P.A. MINNELL

Contents

Introduction and Greetings 7
Māori Spirituality 8
A Quick Note on Māori Pronunciation 11
About the Cards 12
On Working with Your Tūpuna 14
Reading the Cards 17
Whakaaturanga: Sample Readings 19
Karakia Karanga: A Calling Prayer 24
Karakia Poroaki: A Farewell Prayer 25

The Oracle Cards 26

Aruhe, *Roots of the Bracken Fern* 27
Harakeke, *New Zealand Flax* 28
Heru, *Māori Comb* 29
Hoe, *Canoe Paddle* 30
Hōrirerire, *Grey Warbler* 31
Kāhu, *Māori Kite* 31
Kaikōmako, *A Native Tree* 32
Kākahu, *Māori Cloak* 33
Kauri, *Native Conifer* 34
Kawakawa, *New Zealand Peppertree* 35
Kea, *Native Alpine Parrot* 36
Kēkerewai, *Manuka Beetle* 37
Kererū, *Native Wood Pigeon* 37
Kina, *Spiny Sea Egg* 38
Kiwi, *Native Flightless Bird* 39
Kō, *Digging Stick* 40
Koreke, *Native Quail* 41
Koromiko, *Native Shrub* 42
Koru, *Fern Sprout* 43
Kōtarepopo, *Kingfisher* 44
Kōtuku, *White Heron* 45
Kōwhai, *Native Tree* 45
Kūmara, *Sweet Root Vegetable* 46
Mānuka, *Native Tea tree* 47
Mātau, *Fish Hook* 48
Mauri, *Talisman of Life* 49
Mere, *Club Weapon* 50
Mūwharu, *Caterpillar of the Sphinx Moth* .. 51
Namunamu, *Sandfly* 52

Ngārara, *The Little Green Lizard* 53
Pakake, *Whale* 54
Pāpaka, *Crab* 55
Pāua, *Native Abalone* 55
Pīwakawaka, *Native Fantail* 56
Pōhā, *Soft Kelp Bag* 57
Pōhutukawa, *Native Tree* 58
Poi, *Māori Entertainment* 59
Pūrerehua, *Ritual Musical Instrument* 60
Rata, *Ancient Hero* 61
Raupō, *Bulrush/Catail* 62
Ruahine, *Priestess Healer* 63
Ruru, *Native Owl* 64
Tākeke, *The Mesh of the Fishing Net* 65
Taniwha, *River Guardian* 65
Tarāpunga, *Little Red Billed Seagull* 66
Tātarāmoa, *Native Blackberry Vine* 67
Tāwera, *Morning Star* 67
Tī Kōuka, *Cabbage Tree* 68
Tī Rākau, *Stick Game* 69
Tira, *Wand* 69
Toetoe, *Native Sedge Grass* 70
Tōtara, *Native Sonifer* 71
Tuatara, *Native Lizard* 72
Tūī, *Native Parson Bird* 72
Tuna, *Native Eel* 73
Uenuku, *The Rainbow* 74
Waikaka, *Native Mudfish* 75
Wētā Taipo, *Cave Weta* 75

Glossary 77
Bibliography and Recommended Reading 78
About the Author 79

Introduction and Greetings

Tena Koutou Katoa! Greetings to you all!

In almost every culture that exists or has existed, there was once a belief in the presence of those who had passed on and, in most of these traditions, it was also believed that guidance could be sought from them. In many western cultures, a small portion of these beliefs remain, but the bulk of them have fallen by the wayside and, in a modern world, those who have preceded us to the Heavens often feel lost to us.

For the traditional New Zealand Māori, these beliefs are still very strong, and from the bond between the living and the dead comes personal strength and a sense of purpose.

The Māori Oracle is based around the ages-old tradition of consulting the ancestors and employs many of the teaching stories, omens, and portents that were once used by the New Zealand Māori. Once upon a time, these ways were only told to those within the whānau [*family*]. Adaptation to Western society over the last hundred years has meant that, for many Māori families, these precious ways have been all but lost. Today, in New Zealand there is currently a drive towards the recovery and enrichment of Māori culture. And while there are still some who feel that Māori ways should only be taught to Māori, there are many more who believe that its survival lies in simply teaching it to any who want to learn.

In this way, *The Māori Oracle* is an invitation to learn a little bit about Māori language and customs and to understand and share in a small measure the Māori culture. To help people become familiar with the meanings of Māori words, there is an English translation in square brackets directly after most Māori words. Sometimes the meanings will vary though, according to context.

Most importantly, however, *The Māori Oracle* is a reconnection to one's ancestors and to loved ones who have passed on – a reminder, if you will, that they remain to give their help and love when we need it most. Regardless of what symbols and icons are used, the cards themselves are the vehicle of a message – a message in the language of Spirit, a language that is universal.

Māori Spirituality

Although little is commonly known about it, the New Zealand Māori have always had a rich magical tradition. In the old days, the ways of the Whare Wānanga [*Houses of Sacred Learning*] touched on almost every aspect of everyday life. A teacher within the Whare Wānanga was called a Tohunga in the North of New Zealand, and a Tohuka in the South. These men and women were priests, healers, guides, advisors, gardeners, midwives, navigators, weavers, carvers, storytellers, and guardians of the family knowledge and bloodlines. Each and every aspect was sacred to the tribe because it was linked to their very survival.

To the Māori of old, the presence of Tūpuna [*Ancestors*] and Atua [*Gods*] was unquestionable. It is still this way for many – although in an altered fashion for most, with the majority of Māori families converting to Christianity in the nineteenth century.

When looking at old Māori ways, it's important to understand that Māori cosmology is very complex and rich, with the relationship between Tūpuna and Atua blurring frequently. Tūpuna and Atua are not necessarily separate concepts for the New Zealand Māori. Nearly all tribal whakapapa [*family histories*] contain ancestors who became deified in the course of time and are specifically referred to as family Atua. Tribal whakapapa are actually traced back to some of the Greater Gods themselves.

Māori cosmology itself can differ from tribe to tribe, but in most traditions there are ten (sometimes twelve) heavens, all with their own Atua [*gods*], Apa [*servants*] and Kaitiaki [*guardians*]. The nearest heaven to Te Ao Mārama, the earthly realm of mankind, is Ranginui-a-tamaku-rangi, the realm of Ranginui the Sky Father. In the South Island tribes he is known as Rakinui. He had several wives, but the most well-known today is Papatūānuku, the Earth Mother. Between them move their many, many children.

The most commonly known of these are:

- **Haumiatiketike,** the god of wild foods
- **Rongomātāne,** the god of cultivated foods
- **Rūaumoko,** the god of volcanoes
- **Tāne Mahuta,** the god of the forest
- **Tangaroa,** the god of the seas
  (although it should be said that in some tribal traditions, Tangaroa is the husband of Papatūānuku, and not her son)
- **Tāwhiri-mātea,** the god of the winds and tempests
- **Tū matenga,** the god of war
- **Whiro,** the god of sickness and chaos

With the coming of Christianity, family Atua are rarely acknowledged amongst modern Māori today, but traditional Māori have always been acutely aware of the presence of their Tūpuna and have a strong belief that they are cared for by them. In some places, you will still see carvings or representations of the Tūpuna Tūārangi – the ancient ancestors. In the old days, people took great measures to ensure that the Tūpuna and the Atua were not offended. Everything centred on maintaining tapu [*sacred rules of restriction*] correctly, which touched almost every aspect of life, including people, places, food, and objects. Personal tapu was closely guarded, more than anything else, because it was considered that by allowing your personal items to become defiled, you were breaking tapu yourself and incurring the wrath of your own Tūpuna and the Atua. You would never leave your food uneaten (especially as a guest elsewhere) nor spit on the ground, for fear of someone causing it to become defiled and thereby causing you to become cursed. In one area in particular, a war erupted over the wearing of the cloak of an Ariki [*chieftain*], which resulted in the deaths of hundreds of South Island Māori in the early 1800s. Tapu was, and still is, a very serious matter.

Some customs are still very strongly adhered to, in honor of the Tūpuna. The Wharenui, or Whare Tūpuna, has always been one of the most sacred buildings for Māori. It is the central meeting house for a marae [*place of gathering*], kāinga [*village*] or pā [*fort*]. Not only is it the central meeting house, but it is also the tribe's testimony of its whakapapa [*family histories*] and everywhere, inside and outside of a Wharenui, you will find whakairo [*decoration*] depicting the tribes ancestors and deeds. In ancient times, in some tribes, the bones of the Tūpuna would be put into special boxes or baskets and hung high in the rafters. So the Wharenui is literally the house of the ancestors. Because of this, no one eats, smokes, or drinks in a Wharenui or an urupā [*cemetery*]. Neither is it acceptable to wear shoes in a Wharenui. Food is considered a gift of the ancestors and so any place where food sits or is prepared, must never be sat upon. Sitting on tables is considered a great insult to traditional Māori. The head on a person is also sacred because it is considered the seat of a person's ancestral mana [*spiritual strength*] and should not be touched. Special customs surround anything that concerns the head, like pillows or combs. Māori will not sit on pillows intended for the head, nor will they step over a pillow – or a person, for that matter.

Although Māori society has become predominately Christian, the influences of the old Atua, and especially the Tūpuna, are still felt to be everywhere – in the elements, the seasons, the stars, and the world around us. Certain trees, plants, animals, and events have a particular meaning, and guidance from the Tūpuna is sometimes read this way.

Many of the omens and portents are simple, with a favourable or unfavourable answer, but some are quite complex and were born of stories and experiences from ancient times. In each story, there is meaning and a moral to be learnt and heeded, should a similar situation arise.

A Quick Note on Māori Pronunciation

Although there are several dialects within the Māori language, the pronunciation of Māori, in general, is easy and fairly straight forward. The accomplishment in successfully learning to speak Māori is not so much in the pronunciation, but in understanding the conceptual nature of the language. It has been said that every third word in Māori is more concept than word! For example, Matakite means "seeing faces." It can refer literally to the faces of family seen in dreams and visions, but it can also be used to describe contact with one's ancestors.

The Māori Oracle helps to provide an inkling into some of the concepts behind the language, so it would be poor indeed to provide the meanings without providing the way in which the names were pronounced.

A very simple rule to remember is that vowels in the Māori language have a different sound than English vowels.

- A as in far or tar (without the "t")
- E as in air or egg (without the "gg")
- I as in sea (without the "s") or flee (without the "fl")
- O as in oar or thaw (without the "th")
- U as in goo (without the "g") or who (without the "wh")

Of course, there are other sounds that are used in the Māori language. Some are strongly different depending on the area or Iwi [*tribe*], but here you will find the most commonly used dialect, recognised no matter where you are. The sounds special to the Māori language are:

- WH as in far (without the "ar")
- NG as in sing (without the "si")
- R is often pronounced with a half roll of the tongue.

In the south of New Zealand, you will also find that "Ng" has been replaced with "K." This is a soft "K" that is uttered almost in the back of the throat in such a way that it sounds almost like a "G." Lastly, you will see accents above the vowels in some Māori words. The sound of an accented vowel is longer than the normal vowel.

About the Cards

The birds, plants, objects, and stories featured in the cards, are considered by many to be Taonga, or National Treasures. Each Taonga is featured on a green background which imitates the Pounamu, or greenstone, which is essentially New Zealand jade. The Pounamu was very highly prized amongst Māori and one solitary polished piece would be carefully handed down through the generations just as the stories of the Māori have been.

The carved-like patterns featured in the background of the cards have multiple meanings. The outermost border pattern is called "Pākati" and has a dual meaning of protection and prosperity. The second border represents the lashed Raupō that is done across the tops of Waka Mōkihi [*bulrush canoes*], used for travel specifically by the Kāti Māmoe tribe from the South Island of New Zealand, to whom the author belongs. The Mōkihi, still in use today, are the oldest form of transport in New Zealand, and the pattern of the Mōkihi represents the past, travelling the gap of time. These cards are messengers from our past, also travelling the gap of time and so the Raupō lashing is most appropriate as a visual container for each kupu [*message*].

The internal pattern was inspired by a canoe bailer from the Kāti Māmoe tribe and is directly symbolic of successful travel.

Because the purpose of the cards is to provide a means of contact with our Tūpuna, they are considered as "touched" by the Tūpuna. Things "touched" in this way become sacred, and the cards should be treated as such during and after use.

There are a few Māori customs specific to the treatment of sacred objects:

- They mustn't come into contact with cooked food or drink. Cooked food, in Māori lore, has the ability to transfer tapu [*sacred restriction*], effectively lifting the sacredness from an object.
- They mustn't be taken into a kitchen, laundry, bathroom, or toilet. These areas, while important to the household, are common areas, and carrying or leaving a sacred object in them, for Māori, is tantamount to leaving your ancestors' bones in a toilet!
- They shouldn't be handled by anyone but the person they were intended for. Handling objects "touched" by the Tūpuna is much the same as "touching" the Tūpuna themselves. It's simply not good manners to "handle" somebody else's relatives!
- Hands are washed and the head is sprinkled with water after dealing with the sacred.

On Working with Your Tūpuna

In the tradition of the New Zealand Māori, you must be sure to pay your respects and give honour to your Tūpuna before seeking guidance from the cards. It must be your own Tūpuna that you acknowledge, not that of another's bloodline, because it is your Tūpuna who you are tied to, both in body and spirit, and it is their existence of which you are a testament. Your honours belong to them.

Understand that when working with spiritual energy, respect and good intentions are paramount. Tūpuna are not bound to aid you, and in anger, they are capable of causing much strife and sickness. Therefore, be respectful when asking for aid, and when the Māori New Year comes, marked by the rise of Matariki [*The Pleiades star cluster*], remember them. In the Northern Hemisphere, this is around the summer solstice and in the Southern Hemisphere, it's around the winter solstice.

Alternatively, you can remember them at All Hallows, which is held towards the end of October in the Northern Hemisphere and between the end of April and early June in the Southern Hemisphere. All Hallows, a beautiful and dignified festival, is the traditional time for respecting the dead in ethnic religions throughout the world. At All Hallows, it is customary to visit the graveyard where family are buried, to clean the gravestones and leave fresh flowers. Some people also use this time of year to teach their families about their history, and many hold a special meal with a plate set aside for those who have passed on – so that they may partake in the celebration as well. It's nice to remember what their favourite foods were, and when the meal is over, what remains is often left in the garden for "the children of the wild."

At the Māori New Year, Māori will sing and chant to their Tūpuna and leave offerings of food, usually fresh and grown by their own hands. Cooked food was not generally offered to the Tūpuna by Māori because it was noa – free from tapu, and therefore capable of transferring tapu. Having said that much, the use of cooked food in sacred rites is a matter of perception, and food cooked by one's own hand is food often cooked with love and respect. Other offerings commonly used throughout the world are money and flowers; incenses may also be lit. Of course, offerings that are traditional to your own heritage are certainly appropriate, providing they don't contravene the laws of the land or the rights of others.

Bathing before engaging in contact with your Tūpuna is not necessary but it is a matter of politeness. The act of bathing is an act of cleansing which extends to the spirit and the Mauri, the life principle with which we are all infused. Cleansing helps to set our goals clearly and removes clutter that would otherwise confuse our efforts. It also aids in a sense of preparation and ceremony for contact with the Tūpuna. Alternatively, you could meditate, using a series of cleansing breaths to clear your mind and help you to make sure that you are clear in your intent.

Contact with your Tūpuna can be made by simple karakia [*prayer*], or it can involve highly structured ceremonies. Traditional Māori favour fairly strict protocols in every ceremony. They are specific to the time a ceremony is performed, where different people sit, what gender performs the different parts of the ceremony, etc. If you wish to use a more structured kind of ceremony, then it is best to use something that is special to you and your family. Aspects of ceremony can involve the clothing that you choose to wear, the time of day, personal prayers, a special place, or even a personal altar with family photos or icons.

When seeking advice from the Tūpuna, a Tohunga would often use the Tūāhu, an altar of sorts. Always out of doors, but private and enclosed, a traditional Tūāhu is a simple affair, often a mound of dirt, a large stone, or a tree stump, accompanied by stones that represent Atua that are special to the tribe. The Tūāhu was especially sacred because it was the home of the spiritual and the physical representation of a tribe's Mauri, the "life spark" gifted from the Tūpuna and the tribal Atua, that gifted life, health, strength, and wellbeing to the tribe. It was in front of the Tūāhu that offerings of food were buried in the soil, such as Kumara and other fresh foodstuffs.

Another way to honor your Tūpuna that is a little more modern, is a memory wall or family shrine within the home. Even from ancient times Māori have adorned the kāinga [*village*] with carved images of their Tūpuna and named their buildings in honour of them as well. Today, in some homes (and in all Wharenui) you will see a memory wall upon which members of the Hapū [*sub-tribe*] who have passed away are represented. If you have a memory wall or family shrine, you might like to tidy it up and light some incense. Whatever is comfortable for you and appropriate to your family is what is best for you to do.

If elaborate ritual is not your style, then it's not really necessary in this case. What you are aiming to do is create a sense of sacredness with what you are doing, and what is most important is the respect you intend towards your ancestors. You know them better than any other. They are family, after all. What may help you to relax and move into the frame of mind required is personal. Some people find the use of low lighting, gentle sound, and comforting scent a must. By all means, use what is necessary, but let none come to harm through your actions. Your own intent of developing contact with your Tūpuna and your need for answers and guidance are what will guide your karakia and give it strength.

Call them by name. If you are unaware of their individual names, you may simply call to the ancestors of your family or Whakapapa [*bloodline*]. Remember that grandparents, parents, other family members, and even friends who have passed on are also counted amongst your Tūpuna.

Use what language you are most familiar with. Your Tūpuna may have spoken a different language to you but the language of the spirit is the language of the heart – emotion. The language in which the karakia is said matters not, because it is the emotion that truly speaks. What matters is that you intimately understand what you are asking. You can choose to speak your karakia in another language, but will you truly understand what you are saying?

Reading the Cards

The Māori Oracle is an oracle deck that you read for yourself. Remember that when you use the Oracle, you are consciously asking for advice from ancestors and loved ones who have passed on. For each card you select, read and give thought to the story and the meaning that comes with it and then allow your instincts to tell you what your Tūpuna are trying to tell you. However, do try to keep the message pure. That is to say that you must be careful not to mix the message with that which you would prefer it to say. Whatever cards you select are all connected, giving you an answer that ranges across the human psyche.

When you are ready and have made your preparations, breathe in deeply and be calm. Call to your Tūpuna; then shuffle the deck well, while keeping your question firmly in mind. Make your question simple and then voice it.

Cut the cards into three stacks. Each stack represents the three divine sources of knowledge, the Pūtea Wānanga. All knowledge, in Māoridom, is said to come from three baskets called Ngā Pūtea Wānanga. They were obtained from the highest heaven by Tāne with the help of the Kōtuku [*White Heron*], for the benefit of mankind. The names of the baskets vary from tribe to tribe, but they are commonly called Te Kete Aronui, Te Kete Tūātea, and Te Kete Tuauri.

The order in which you have cut the cards has no bearing, but whichever stack you set as the first, second, or third basket of knowledge is what is important. And so you need to select a card from each "basket," but each time you select a card, you must be consciously aware of which basket you are drawing from.

The first basket, Te Kete Aronui, is the knowledge of the physical world. So, the first card that you select is the card that talks about the physical world for you. It relates to physical needs, what is physically affecting you, what you physically need to do, and what is physically real for you.

The second basket, Te Kete Tūātea, is the knowledge of ceremonies, customs, laws, and what is right and just. A card from the second basket relates to what we know we should be doing, to what will help us stay on the right path, to what inspires us and teaches us. It is a card that can also relate to the emotions because it also represents what is emotionally real for you.

The third basket is a difficult one. Te Kete Tuauri relates to knowledge that is concealed – magical knowledge, spiritual knowledge, and the world which you cannot see. It can relate to a possible future or a lost past. It can relate to the spiritual powers affecting you, or it can relate to self-deception. Are you disconnected? Are you at war with yourself and perhaps others? Is it your habit to ignore things in the hope they'll go away? It may be an answer that you already know, but have been choosing to ignore. Only you will know that answer, if you have the courage to be honest with what you see.

Every card talks about what you need to consciously be aware of. In each answer lies its meaning and its significance, but also its lessons and its nature, as a talisman. Every card is connected to the others and relates not only to the different aspects of each question, but to the different aspects of ourselves – the spiritual, the physical, and the emotional.

When you have completed your reading, sincerely thank your Tūpuna for their gift of guidance and give to them your offering. It might be a nice thing for you to leave any offerings of food outside for the children of the wild to partake in as well.

After you have given your honours to your Tūpuna, take one very deep breath and release it. Then wash your hands and face in clean water. It is Māori custom to wash the hands and face after dealing with the sacred. It is a large part of the closing ritual for Māori, and prevents the sacred from moving into common life. In this way, the sacred remains sacred.

Whakaaturanga Sample Readings

Reading Number One

First card: Mauri

Because this card was drawn from the first basket – the basket of the physical world – it tells the individual that what she has physically is enough for her. However, the card of Mauri reminds her most importantly that all is connected throughout the physical, emotional, and spiritual realities.

Second card: Koru

The card of family, or more accurately: what makes a family. In this case, the individual was bothered by the idea that what she felt to be family wasn't the normal view of what a family should be. The card strongly suggests that there is no such thing as "the normal family" and that what she had as a family was enough and perfectly acceptable for her. Again, it was a message that she already had, what she actually needed.

Third card: Waikaka

Sometimes, in our distress, we make more of a situation than is really the case. The Waikaka teaches this individual that things are not as bad as they seem, and that if she is smart, she will manage, however which way she can until things come right. And they will come right.

Looking at How It All Comes Together...

Clearly, not all is as bad as it feels. Things can be made worse by focusing on what is not in this individual's life as opposed to what is. Sometimes in a quest to be happy, she may miss that which is already in front of her, already giving her what she needs. Social preconditioning and family ways, or behaviours, can also limit growth, but eventually she must go past them to be where she wants to be.

Reading Number Two

First card: Pāpaka

The question asked by the individual of her ancestors was, "Do we try to stay in the home we're in for another year?" The card of the Pāpaka, coming from the first basket of knowledge, suggests that the individual has perhaps too much attachment to the physical house in which she lives. This can be for many reasons. In this case, the individual feels insecure with moving and almost dreads it. The card of the Pāpaka also suggests that moving on is a good thing, a growing thing, and an opportunity to improve her circumstances.

Second card: Koreke

A card from the second basket of knowledge talks of emotional involvements, as well as duty and custom. When the card of the Koreke comes through, it talks of the need to be truthful with oneself and to be as you must. Sometimes decisions are made more out of a sense of duty, than what is really necessary. And sometimes that sense of duty is what is more comfortable to us; but is it what we need? Could this individual's choice to choose duty and security be limiting her chances to go forward? When the Koreke shows itself, it tells her that it is time to examine the real reasons for staying where she is.

Third card: Ruahine

The card of the Ruahine from the third basket suggests a war with oneself. The Ruahine's message is simple – in truth, nothing holds her back. What she has come to believe is limiting her movement forward and is not real. If she wants to do something, then she should do it – she can, if she chooses to.

Looking at How It All Comes Together...

Limitations in this individual's case appear to be self-imposed, through reasons of family obligation, loyalty, and security. But her choice to stay where she is, is perhaps not what she already knows she needs to do. Her reasons, while honorable and very human, are little but a diversion. Her dreams and aspirations are possible, but only if she has the courage to move forward.

Reading Number Three

First card: Kōwhai

The question asked was, "What's holding us back?" The first card to be drawn was the Kōwhai. The Kōwhai talks of self-belief – believing in your own abilities, holding your head up and being proud of who you are. Often, what holds people back is a self-defeating belief that their dreams are not possible or undeserved. Positive belief in themselves can take these individuals just about anywhere. This card asks them to believe they can and things will come together for them.

Second card: Pīwakawaka

The Pīwakawaka is a guide in Tane's great forest and when the Pīwakawaka comes through in a reading, it means that a way will be found – that what is being sought will come your way – you will prevail. The Pīwakawaka brings with it a sense of destiny, and it is also being suggested that these individuals are worrying unnecessarily.

Third card: Poi

A task taken too seriously becomes much harder than it needs to be. Relax, go with the flow of how things are, and learn to sing while working. This is the message of the Poi. It is why there have always been miners' songs, fishermen's songs, haymakers' songs, and harvesters' songs. This is all hard work, but it all seems much easier when people are relaxed with a song in their hearts.

Looking at How It All Comes Together...

The gentleman asking this question has been through some very difficult times in his past. Sometimes when life has become particularly hard we can come to believe that the difficulties in our lives have no end and that struggle is simply the way things will always be. It's not hard to understand that harsh thoughts towards others have energy and that the energy returns to its source many times over. But the same is even more true with harsh thoughts towards ourselves. Negative thinking habits towards ourselves are often our worst enemies. Although we are often responsible for where we are in life – because we choose to remain where we know the rules – the things that happen to us in life aren't always our own fault, and people rarely deserve bad fortune.

This reading advises that he should change the language he uses towards himself and others involved with the question and the way he views himself. It would be wise to attempt to understand that sometimes a person can just get caught up in someone else's dance.

Karakia Karanga
A Calling Prayer

Karanga ana ahau ki Ngā Tūpuna
o āku whakapapa,
koutou ana tīaho ki te Korowai ō Ranginui,
koutou ana puritia te mātauranga ō āku whānau
Me te aroha me te kauanuanu,
Tēnā koutou tēnā koutou tēnā koutou katoa.
Me te aroha me te kauanuanu,
e whakamori ana ahau.
E rapa atu ana ahau mō
Ngā koha a tō ārahitanga,
kia ka āhei ahau ki te tāwhai te ara ariari
i te wā te hikoi ō tōku ora.

I call to the ancestors of my bloodline,
You who shine from the cloak of Ranginui,
You who hold the wisdom of my family.
With love and respect, I greet you.
With love and respect, I honour you.
I ask for the gift of your guidance,
That I may travel a clearer path
in my life's journey.

Karakia Poroaki
A Farewell Prayer

Me aroha me whakanuia me mihi,
He whakamihi ki a koutou
Ngā Tūpuna ō āku whakapapa,
e nohoia ana a koutou i roto i tōku ngākau.
Hoki atu ki te Karanga ō Hinenuītepo,
e moe marie.
Ka maumahara tonu ki a koutou.
Haere, haere, haere.

With love, with respect, with gratitude,
I thank you.
Ancestors of my blood,
You live within my heart.
Return to the call of Hinenuītepo,
Sleep in peace.
I will remember you.
Farewell, farewell, farewell.

The Oracle Cards

Aruhe

(Pronounced ar-roo-hee)
Roots of the Bracken Fern

DEPENDABILITY. HAVE FAITH.

Aruhe is the gift of Haumiatiketike, the god of wild foods. It was once a staple food for Māori all over New Zealand and nothing was so worthy of trust than the Aruhe. No matter what happened, no matter what crops had failed, nor birds had fled, there would always be Aruhe. And Rarauhe [*bracken*], from which Aruhe is taken, grew also where the favoured Kumara could not. The best Aruhe, which was crisp and white on the inside, was dug up, dried, soaked, roasted in the fire, and then pounded with a club until it made a dough. Then it would be flavoured with other foods, like fish, berries, or nectar to make Kōmeke – a cake-like food of travellers and warriors.

Harakeke

(Pronounced har-raa-qe-qe)
New Zealand Flax

A favourable outcome.

    The Harakeke is a sacred plant and its uses, for the Māori, are almost unending. Its name means hold fast, and as a fibre, there was nothing that matched it. The leaves are woven into mats, ropes, baskets, sandals, packs, hats, and many other things. They can also be stripped down into a much finer fibre, called muka, and used to make clothing. It was traditionally gathered by the women for these uses, but never while they were menstruating, pregnant, or feeding babies. As a medicine, its uses are also widely varied, from wounds to constipation.

    There is a very special way in which to gather the leaves of the Harakeke. The young shoots come up from the protective inside of the older shoots. The newest shoot is seen as "the child," the next layer of leaves going outwards are "the parents" and the oldest on the outside are "the grandparents." Usually, one would gather from "the grandparent" leaves. With one exception, one should never pick the young middle shoot, the rito, as it risks damaging the plant. On rare occasions, it was sometimes picked to foretell victory or failure for an expedition, usually a war expedition. If the bottom broke evenly and straight when plucked from the bush, it was a sign of victory to come.

Heru

(Pronounced hear-roo)
Māori Comb

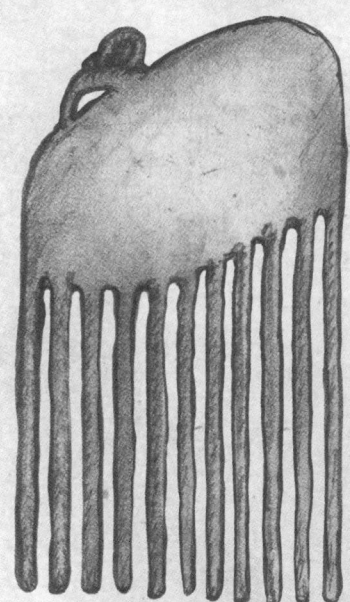

EGO. DO NOT LET THE EGO DESTROY YOUR GOAL.

For Māori, the head is one of the most sacred parts of the body and anything that ordinarily touches the head retains the sacredness of the person they belong to. Consequently, a Heru is also a sacred thing, and in olden times, it was also an indication of status and was worn by the Rangatira [*highborn*].

There are a number of stories that involve a Heru. One in particular tells of two Ariki [*chieftains*] who were having an argument: One who honoured the old ways and paid homage to the Māori Atua [*Māori Gods*], and the other who had converted to another religion. They were trying to disprove the power of the other's Atua. Sadly, the Ariki of the old ways sought to win through trickery, but in doing so, he had admitted to Hara, which is the crime of breaking tapu.

When someone has been careless enough to allow something such as a comb to be taken and corrupted, they have allowed their "tapu" and that of their ancestors to be corrupted, and so it is they who have committed the Hara – not the person who "took the comb and destroyed its sacredness."

And so in his eagerness to win, he forgot the teachings of his ancestors and he failed.

Hoe

(Pronounced haw-air)
Canoe Paddle

MIGRATION, TRAVEL, CHANGE. WORK TO WHERE YOU WANT TO GO.

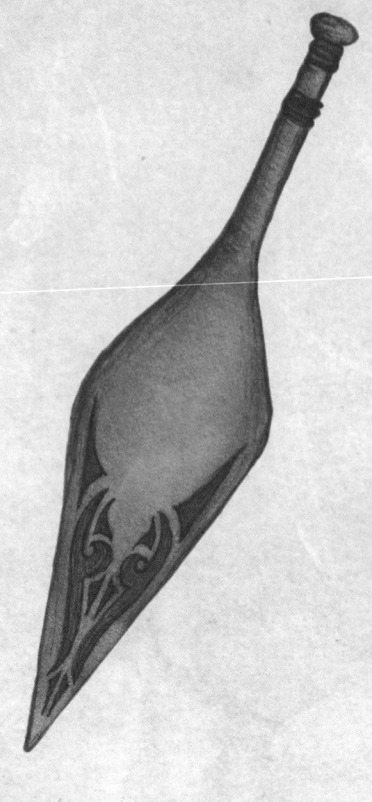

The New Zealand Māori people are not indigenous to Aotearoa [*New Zealand*]. All Tūpuna came by canoe and sailed from different places – most from Hawaikī-nui. The names of the canoes upon which they arrived are still retained in some of the names of the tribes to this day. The seemingly unimportant Hoe and a great deal of awe [*might*] brought the Māori to this land of plenty over 500 years ago.

What is interesting to note is that, no matter how big the canoe, one goes nowhere without effort.

Hōrirerire

(Pronounced haw-ree-rare-ree-rare)
Grey Warbler

PREPARE.
LAZY PEOPLE GO HUNGRY IN WINTER.

The Hōrirerire is also known as the Riroriro and it heralds the spring, announcing that it is time to prepare the ground and plant the crops. Or more precisely, it is the sound of the nemesis of the Hōrirerire that heralds the spring! When you hear the distinctive four-note call of the Pīpīwharauroa [*the Shining Cuckoo*], you know that the Hōrirerire is about to be a foster parent. But it is so organised in its nestmaking, that when the Pīpīwharauroa arrives to leave its egg in the Hōrirerire's nest, the Hōrirerire has already raised its children.

A good harvest is born of careful preparation and without action at the right time, the best harvest is not possible. And so it is with many things.

Kāhu

(Pronounced caa-hoo)
Māori kite

TRUTH WILL FIND ITS WAY.
WHAT WAS HIDDEN COMES TO LIGHT.

The name of the Kāhu, or the hawk, is also the name of the Māori kite. Kites were made of many things, but often of Raupō [*Bulrushes*]. A Tohunga would send up a Kāhu with karakia [*prayer*], seeking to enlist the aid of the spirits and the Atua of the winds. He would do this to discover the direction or position of those who had committed wrongful acts, such as theft or murder. They would also use it to find something hidden or lost, or to suggest a path of travel.

Kaikōmako

(Pronounced kae-caw-maa-caw)
A Native Tree

Take heart. All is never lost.

Its Latin name is *Pennantia Corymbosa* and it is endemic to New Zealand. The Kaikōmako is one of five very special trees in that it helped Mahuika, the Goddess of fire, to save fire for the use of humankind forever.

Maui, a descendant of Mahuika herself, was a very mischievous man. To find out where fire came from, he put out all the fires of his people one night. When it was discovered, he volunteered to retrieve some more. He was sent to Mahuika, who kept her flame children concealed within her fingernails and toenails.

Upon hearing that humankind was without fire, she removed one of her precious fingernails and gave it to Maui, warning him to keep it safe on his journey back. As soon as he was out of sight, he extinguished the flame and then went back to ask for more. He did this many times. Almost too late, Mahuika discovered Maui's mischief and, in a rage, she sent the last of the children after him, to punish him.

The fire consumed everything in its pursuit of Maui. To escape, Maui transformed himself into a Kahu [*hawk*] while calling to Tāwhiri-mātea, the god of tempests, who dowsed the roaring flames with rain.

Mahuika, realising that the last of her children were about to be extinguished, appealed to the trees to hide them from the rains. Only five, out of all the great forests of Tane, answered her plea: the Tōtara, the Pukatea, the Patete, the Māhoe, and the Kaikōmako.

To this day, you will still find fire hiding in any one of these woods by rubbing a kaurimarima [*pointed stick of a hardwood tree*] into a kauati [*grooved fire-tree wood*], especially the Kaikōmako.

Kākahu

(Pronounced caa-caa-hoo)
Māori Cloak

PURPOSE. BY LOOKING AHEAD, YOU CAN WORK YOUR WAY THROUGH WHAT MUST BE DONE NOW.

When a weaver sits down to make a Kākahu it is a sacred act, more often for a member of her Hapū [*sub-tribe*], rarely for herself. She knows that she has many months of work ahead of her, involving many processes and observing many traditions.

Harakeke [*New Zealand Flax*] is collected, soaked, stripped, beaten, rubbed, and bleached in the sun to become muka, a fine, soft fibre. Sometimes the muka is dyed to provide coloured weaving material for the cloak and its decorative borders. Creating the dyes also takes a considerable amount of time. After all the preparation has been done and the materials gathered, the weaving begins. And when the weaving is done, the blessings begin.

In the old days, the wearing of a cloak was certainly about prestige, but mostly about survival, providing warmth in the cold months and an advantage in battle (a closer weave slows the sharp blade). A weaver also knows that the cloak will not remain with the person for whom it is made. It will be passed down through the whānau [*family*] for generations to come. So when a weaver weaves a Kākahu, she weaves with the purpose and dedication of providing for the generations ahead.

If a weaver was to set her mind on only the tasks ahead of her, the process of making a Kākahu could come to feel monumental and overbearing. But instead, by seeing the completed Kākahu in her mind, the work becomes a thing of joy.

Kauri

(Pronounced cow-ree)
Native Conifer

STAND STRONG. STAND TRUE.

The oldest and largest of New Zealand native trees was named Tāne Mahuta, in honour of the God of the Forests, and it was a Kauri. This honor goes back to the legend of the separation of Papatūānuku [*the Earth Mother*] and Ranginui [*the Sky Father*]. They were so much in love with each other that their embrace was neverending. Very romantic, but for those who lived between them, it meant a neverending taipōuri or darkness.

It was eventually decided by the children of Papatūānuku and Ranginui that their parents would have to be separated to allow light to come back into the world. Many things were tried, but nothing worked until Tāne Mahuta, the god of the forests, decided to try. Bracing his shoulders against the earth, he placed his mighty feet against the sky and pushed until his parents were separated. And so it was that Te Ao Mārama, the world of light, was born.

Kawakawa

(Pronounced caa-waa-caa-waa)
New Zealand Peppertree

CHANGE. A NECESSARY TRANSITION FROM ONE STATE TO ANOTHER.

Kawakawa is used for cleansing and a clearing of the ways, both in a physical and a spiritual sense. It is an extremely valuable medicinal plant and it is said that where the Kawakawa grows, a family will be well. In the past, the twigs of the Kawakawa were used by the Tohunga to lift Tapu [*sacred restriction*] and in many ceremonies. Today, it is often waved by the women at any event where a Pōwhiri [*welcoming of visitors*] is performed and it is still used at Tangihanga [*funerals*], woven into Tauā [*mourning head wreaths*] as well. When the Kawakawa is worn at a tangi it is to help both the living and the dead to heal and move on.

Kea

(Pronounced key-yaa)
Native Alpine Parrot

BOLDNESS, EXPLORATION.
FEAR NOT A CHANGE IN YOUR "LANDSCAPE."

The Kea is possibly the cheekiest bird you will ever meet. Around New Zealand, you will find frequent signs asking not to feed them and warnings about their thieving and destructive habits. Wild birds are more than happy to accept titbits from anyone and are known for tearing pieces off your car.

When old-time Māori went in search of Pounamu [*Greenstone/Jade*] and other treasured resources, they would know where to look if ever two Kea were seen to fly overhead. Few have the true explorer's gift of māia [*boldness*] to discover unknown territory without the trepidation that holds most back. But it is with bold exploration that the greatest treasures, both within oneself and without, can be uncovered.

Kēkerewai

(Pronounced qe-qe-rare-why)
Manuka Beetle

SOME OF YOUR WAYS MAY BE KEEPING YOU WHERE YOU DON'T WANT TO BE.

Keke means stubborn, and the Kēkerewai is so reluctant to change its ways, that it is known for flying into mud banks rather than change its flight path.

Unfortunately for the Kēkerewai, it was once a favoured food for Māori and its failings allowed it to be caught and killed easily.

Kererū

(Pronounced qe-rare-roo)
Native Wood Pigeon

**UNSEEN COMPANY.
YOU DO NOT STAND ALONE.**

For the Māori, death is not a permanent separation. When called or needed, loved ones who have passed away are still there, guiding and loving, as before. Often, they choose to appear in various physical forms, especially birds and particularly the Kererū for many whānau [*families*]. When a bird is believed to carry the messages of loved ones from the other side, it is called an Atua bird.

The approval of the ancestors is said to be given through the call of the Kererū. If the Kererū is heard at the moment of a boy childs' birth, it is a sign of a significant life to come, and many a wedding or special event has been attended by the Kererū.

Kina

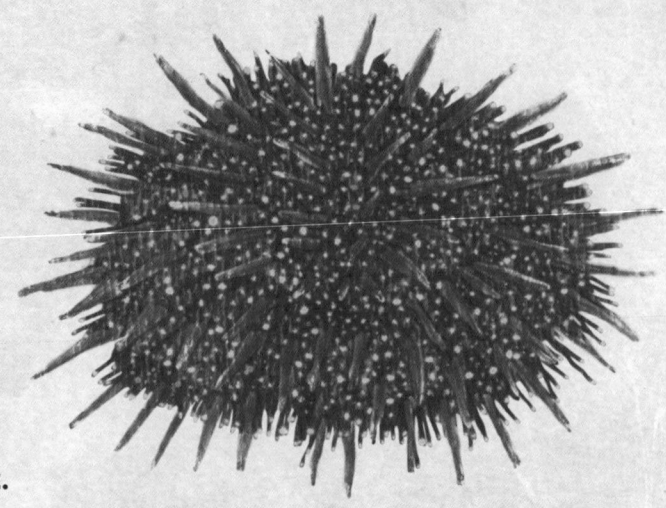

(Pronounced kee-naa)
Spiny Sea Egg

**EVERYTHING HAS
ITS TIME AND PLACE.**

    Kaimoana [*seafood*] holds a special place for Māori and favoured fishing spots are treasured for generations. Even in ancient times, inland Māori would travel miles to trade with coastal Māori.
    Kina is one of the many delicacies from the sea and is sought after throughout Raumati [*summer*], but there is a small window of time when the Kina are at their very best, if you can wait. From the time of the blooming Kōwhai you can eat them, but they won't be nearly as nice as if you waited till the bright red Pōhutakawa flowers have arrived. Even so, they are best taken at low tide on certain days between Rakaunui, the day after the full moon, and three days before Whiro, the day of the dark moon.

Kiwi

(Pronounced key-wee)
Native Flightless Bird

SACRIFICE FOR THE GREATER GOOD.
TRY TO SEE THE BIGGER PICTURE.

    Noble and forward thinking beyond measure, the Kiwi was the only bird to answer a call of help from Tāne, the God of the Forest, when the bugs were eating his children, the trees. Only the Kiwi could see that, without the trees, the birds above would have no homes at all one day and so he gave up his beautiful plumage and his splendid wings that he might live on the ground in the dark of the forest, eating the bugs that plagued the trees.

Kō

(Pronounced caw)
Digging Stick

ABUNDANCE WILL BE YOURS WITH TIME AND HARD WORK.

No matter where the Māori lived in the old days, whether it be Pā [*fort*] or kāinga [*village*], there was always a Māra – a vegetable garden. In the vegetable garden was always Kūmara [*sweet potato*] and Taewa [*Māori potato*]. Nothing happened in the gardens without the turning of the soil by the Kō.

Hard work, but the harvests in the end are worth it.

Koreke

(Pronounced caw-rare-qe)
Native Quail

SELF-TRUTH. BE AS YOU MUST.

An old story from the South Island of New Zealand teaches that in one's own personal universe, one must walk the path that is best for him or her. The Koreke was very close friends with the Pakake [*the seal*] and each tried to convince the other to come and live where he preferred to be. The Pakake finally stated that he was going to live in the sea and turned to go. The Koreke pleaded with him to stay, but he said that if he stayed, he would be too easy to kill and would be killed for his meat. And so after a difficult farewell, the two separated forever – the Koreke to the land, and the Pakake to the sea.

Koromiko

(Pronounced caw-raw-mee-caw)
Native Shrub

**TAKE CARE THAT THE FUTURE HOLDS
AS MUCH REGARD AS THE PRESENT.**

    Koromiko holds a special place, similar to that of the Kawakawa, and it is used in many Māori ceremonies, both for the living and the dead. It is its reputation for healing that it is best known for, and Koromiko has been used in the world of Western medicine, as well as the world of the Māori. This reputation was so great that it was sent overseas to cure dysentery amongst New Zealand troops in both World Wars.
    In the south of New Zealand it is still very special, but when the Koromiko crackles in the fire, people believe that all can be seen of the Moa is the grease left behind on the Koromiko leaves. The Moa was a giant bird, perhaps similar to the Emu. It was a great resource for the Māori – perhaps too great, for it is now believed to be extinct.

Koru

(Pronounced caw-roo)
Fern Sprout

FAMILY, SECURITY. LIFE IS PRECIOUS; NURTURE IT IN EVERY WAY.

Emerging from the very centre of the fern, it steadily unfolds while keeping its youngest and most tender leaves safe within its curl. This is the Koru, the symbol of family. It represents the preciousness of children, the cycles of life and the sanctity of family. For Māori, much emphasis is placed on the importance of whānau [*family*]. There are many different types of families – not all are ngare [*related by blood*]. They are a family by what a family truly provides…nurturing, security, and love.

Kōtarepopo

(Pronounced caw-taa-rare-paw-paw)
Kingfisher

UNDERESTIMATION. THE NATURE OF A THING OUTSIDE ITSELF MAY NOT ALWAYS REFLECT ITS TRUTH.

The Kōtarepopo is a beautiful bird, not much bigger than a blackbird. However, it has the reputation of a fierce unflinching warrior, despite its size. One legend tells of the death of a Tui, impaled upon the beak of the Kōtarepopo; another of a hawk with the same fate. It has been known to take on cats and other animals that would otherwise cause terror in other birds. Its manner of attack is by no means careless and it has a hunting style that can only be called "studied." The Kōtarepopo will sit in plain view, seemingly unconcerned with the business of survival, perfectly visible to its intended prey, and when the time is right and its prey has given away all its secrets, then it will quite suddenly strike. It is also a champion of the light, in that it also preys upon the lizards – the servants of Whiro, the God of Sickness, Darkness, and Chaos.

Kōtuku

(Pronounced caw-two-koo)
White Heron

THE FAVOUR OF THE GODS. HAVE FAITH.

Legend says that it was upon the back of the Kōtuku that Tāne rode up to Tikitiki-o-ngā-rangi, the highest of Heavens, in order to obtain the three sacred baskets of knowledge.

Only something so pure could gain passage past all the guardians of the houses leading to and from the other Heavens.

So it is that the Kōtuku is a symbol of all that is blessed. Pure, graceful, and beautiful, the Kōtuku is a sign that you are on the right path.

Kōwhai

(Pronounced caw-fai)
Native tree

SELF BELIEF.
BE BOLD, BE PROUD, AS YOU MUST BE.

Called Kōhai in the South of New Zealand, the Kōwhai is New Zealand's national flower. It is one of the few New Zealand trees to shed its leaves over Winter, and flowers before the new leaves have sprung. Legend says that the Kōwhai has flowered in this way ever since a young Tohunga caused it to flower too early in order to meet the challenges of his intended bride.

Bold and proud, as it must be to attract the birds that pollinate it, the Kōwhai has the brightest flowers in the New Zealand bush. Bold and proud, it must be, for when the Kōwhai blooms, it marks the time to start planting Kūmera.

Kūmara

(Pronounced koo-maa-raa)
Sweet Root Vegetable

PEACE AND PLENTY.
THE FRUITS OF YOUR LABOURS ARRIVE.

As one of the staple foods of the Māori, the Kūmara is matahīapo [*prized*], and Māra Kūmara [*Kūmara gardens*] have been kept by the Māori for over a thousand years, both for food and for sacred purposes. It is sacred to Rongomātāne, the God of Agriculture and peace, and because it is the symbol of peace and happiness, it was often offered as a gift by visitors. It was also customary to take a basket of Kūmara when visiting someone for the first time. The lifting of the Kūmara crop, which is done between the autumn equinox and the winter solstice (depending on tribal tradition), is a time of great joy, festivity, and ceremony. Traditional Māori greet the rise of Matariki [*the Pleiades*] at dawn with karakia [*salutations and prayer*] and then lift Te Maomaoa, the first Kūmara (that had also been the first to be planted), which should always be given back to Rongomātāne. Then the harvest begins!

Mānuka

(Pronounced maa-noo-kaa)
Native Tea tree

Adaptability.

    Mānuka has been called the Tea tree since the time of Captain Cook, a European explorer of the late eighteenth century. Settlers and sailors would boil the leaves and bark to make an alternative to tea. The Māori used it as an antiseptic treatment for all manner of ailments, inside and out of the body.
    Manuka grows anywhere and is the tree that grows where no others have been able to thrive. The smallest of Manuka seedlings will not only become tall and strong, weathering the wildest of storms, but its children will eventually cover the hill upon which it stands.

Mātau

(Pronounced maa-tow)
Fish Hook

**OPPORTUNITY BORN
OF DETERMINATION.
WITH DILIGENCE AND PATIENCE,
YOU WILL BENEFIT.**

    A good fisherman knows that to catch any one type of fish, you need to fish with the right bait, in a particular place, at a particular time. Sometimes it can take a long time to work out these variables. And even then, you must be patient and persevere. In doing so, eventually abundance will be yours.

Mauri

(Pronounced maw-oo-ree)
Talisman of Life

ABUNDANCE AND FERTILITY. ALL HAS ITS PURPOSE AND ALL IS CONNECTED.

Mauri exists everywhere there is life – in the forest, in the earth, in the sea, and in everything that lives and breathes. It is the divine life energy that connects everything. The first seeds to be sown and the first root crops to be planted were considered the living representatives of Mauri – the life force that would be gifted to the whole of the crops and, in turn, the whole of humankind. Because of this gift, the Maomaoa [*first Kumara*], the Tūāpora [*first fruits*], and the Taitai [*first catch*] were always given back to their respective Gods. In doing this, it ensures that the gift of life can be continually provided. Sometimes a Tohunga would imbue a Taonga [*tribal treasure*] with the essence of Mauri, and that would then become the physical presence of abundance for the tribe.

Mere

(Pronounced mare-re)
Club Weapon

CHALLENGES, DIFFICULTIES, CONFLICT.
PLAN YOUR APPROACH.

    Although the mere is the symbol of battle, it is always important to first choose carefully the manner in which you fight and the battleground upon which you choose to stand. It is no mistake that the most valued of Māori warriors have been the most cunning. Not all warriors charge their opponents, weapons in hand, and not all battles are fought on the battlefield. Many a seemingly hopeless situation has been won through wit and cunning. Careful planning will aid you in winning on your own ground.

Mūwharu

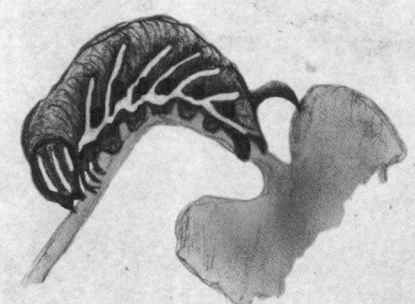

(Pronounced moo-far-roo)
Caterpillar of the Sphinx Moth

**NEGLECT. IN YOUR PASSION,
DO NOT FORGET YOUR RESPONSIBILITIES.**

    Pourangahua was a Matapaheru, a Tohunga who specialises in the care of the Kūmara. He was sent to Aotearoa by an Ariki named Ruakapanga to investigate the growing conditions for the Kūmara. Because his findings were so favourable, Ruakapanga sent him back in great haste to plant the Kūmara in time for the planting season. To do this, he lent him two of his most beloved pets, Harongarangi and Tiungarangihei, two great albatrosses. In his excitement, Pourangahua neglected their care and had to send them home in a shameful state. Naturally, Ruakapanga took great offence and consequently sent the Mūwharu and other insects, which still plague the Kūmara today.

Namunamu

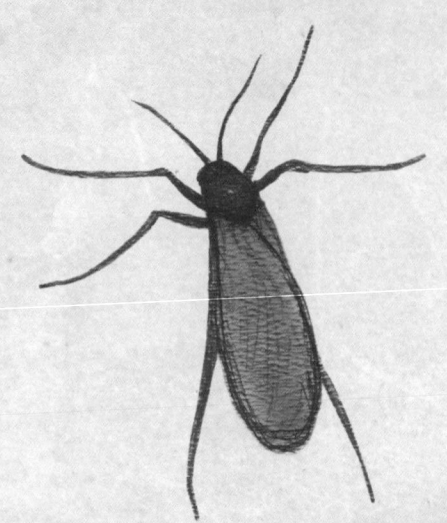

(Pronounced naa-moo-naa-moo)
Sandfly

A SMALL NUISANCE.
IT IS UNREASONABLE TO EXPECT PERFECTION.

Māori legend says that Papatuanuku [*the Earth Mother*] and Ranginui [*the Sky Father*] once lay so close together that the world was always dark. Their sons decided that to allow light into the world, the two would have to be separated, and so they pushed them apart. Light flooded into the world and Te Ao Mārama [*the earthly realm*] came into being. This made life much easier for all living on earth, but Papatuanuku was left very bare and this, combined with the loss of her husband, left her weeping. So Tangaroa spread about the seas, Tane his forests and trees, and Te-Iho-Rangi the snows. After a good while, this left their mother clothed in many beautiful hues of green, blue, and white.

So wonderful was their world that it was feared that the land had become too beautiful for man to live in and that some Gods were bound to take it back for themselves. So Ngā Namunamu, the sandflies, were brought into being.

Ngārara

(Pronounced naa-raa-raa)
The Little Green Lizard

SICKNESS. TAKE BETTER CARE OF YOURSELF AND ALLOW THOSE AROUND YOU TO KNOW THEIR PRECIOUSNESS.

In times past, people would try to kill the small green lizard, if it was ever to cross their paths. This was because it was said to be the physical representation of the God of evil, Whiro, who reigns during the black moon. For some families, it is also an omen of death for a family member, if not a serious illness.

Whiro became angry with his brother, Tāne, who had ascended to the highest heavens before him. It was a matter of courtesy and protocol in his view. He felt that, as the older brother, it was his right before Tāne. From then on, he was the enemy of humankind, who were the children of Tāne. When sickness and bad luck persists, it is sometimes believed to come from Whiro and his family.

Pakake

(Pronounced paa-kaa-qe)
Whale

FRIENDSHIP.
SEEK THE COMFORT OF FRIENDS.

In ancient times, the bonds of friendship were very strong between man and whale. The whale was Kaitiaki [*guardian*], guide and friend to many a tribe. Their friendships were sacred, as were they, and their names are well remembered. So strong were these bonds that often they surpassed death.

According to legend, Paikea, a very famous Tūpuna, arrived in New Zealand on the back of a whale named Tahora, who rescued him from drowning. On another occasion, the murder of the whale, Tutunui, was an immediate call to war. In Kaikōura, the descendants of Te Rakaitauneke still look out for the descendants of his friend, the whale, Matamata. For this reason, many Māori face the sea with confidence because of these age-old legacies.

Pāpaka

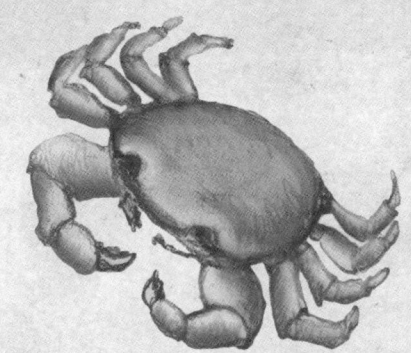

(Pronounced paa-paa-kaa)
Crab

RENEWAL. A NEW BEGINNING IS AN OPPORTUNITY FOR IMPROVEMENT.

The pāpaka is the symbol of Turakautahi, one of the greatest Ariki of the Ngāi Tahu tribe. It is said that the symbol of the crab represents the tribe's battle technique, but it also represents the tribe's ability to renew itself, as does a crab when it outgrows its shell. Many times in history have most tribes been forced to leave and start over elsewhere. And many times have they succeeded, finding better places to be, finding greater strength within.

Pāua

(Pronounced paa-oo-waa)
Native Abalone

BE STAUNCH, BUT NOT BLIND.

The Pāua are known for their tenacity and strength, as well as their beauty. Through the strongest lashing they will keep to their chosen spot, clinging to the rocks, despite the worst of Tangaroa's storms. However, if you shell them and eat them where you find them, that spot will become wāhi-mahue [*deserted*]. The Pāua will abandon their homes, knowing a true enemy when they see it.

Pīwakawaka

(Pronounced pee-waa-kaa-waa-kaa)
Native Fantail

THE GUIDE. A WAY WILL BE FOUND.

Most Māori know the Pīwakawaka as an omen of death, and it is believed that if the Pīwakawaka flies into a house, someone in that household is about to die. But the Pīwakawaka is an Atua bird – that is to say, it is a form that the spirits (Gods or ancestors) often take, and the nature of the omen will depend upon the color of his tail. He is messenger, guide, and the first sentry to pass as you enter Tāne's domain. He will approach you to discover your intentions, and if you are lost, some believe he may lead you to safety. Legend says that his tail became fanned out as it is today, when Māui (a demi god) squeezed him to find the whereabouts of Mahuika, the Goddess of Fire. The Pīwakawaka was to have his revenge when he accompanied Māui on a later expedition — a quest to kill the Goddess of Death, Hine-nui-te-po. At the crucial moment, Pīwakawaka laughed. Hine-nui-te-po awoke and crushed Māui between her thighs.

Pōhā

(Pronounced paw-haa)
Soft Kelp Bag

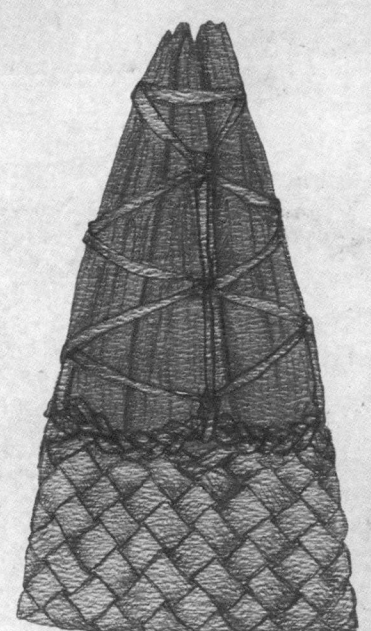

A JOURNEY WITHOUT PREPARATION IS A JOURNEY THAT BECOMES HARDER THAN IT NEEDS TO BE.

Around late autumn every year, Murihiku Māori, at the bottom of the South Island, travel across from Rakiura [*Stewart Island*] for the Hoputītī – the harvest of the Tītī [*muttonbirds*]. These birds are preserved in their own fat within Pōhā before returning home.

Making Pōhā is a lengthy process. A piece of Rimurapa [*great Bull Kelp*] is collected and hollowed out with the hands. Then it's tied with muka [*fibre made from the Harakeke*] at the mouth, blown up with a Pupuhi-rimu [*blowing tube*], and hung in the sun to dry. After a few days, the Pōhā is worked on, using various methods to make it soft and elastic. When the Pōhā is ready, a protective covering is woven around it, using bark and Harakeke.

Indeed, it is a lengthy process, but it is said that a well-made Pōhā will successfully preserve its contents for up to two years.

Pōhutukawa

(Pronounced paw-hoo-too-caa-waa)
Native Tree

**DO NOT FAIL TO VALUE
THAT WHICH YOU ALREADY HAVE.**

When the canoe of the Te Arawa people came into sight of Aotearoa in the fourteenth century, beautiful Pōhutukawa trees in full bloom were seen along the coast.

One of the Ariki, Tauninihi, stood up in wonder and, thinking that the flowers of the Pōhutukawa would be better, discarded Taiwhakaea, his headdress of red feathers. Upon gaining some of the flowers of the Pōhutukawa, he was sad to find that the flowers wilted and died too quickly to be used. He did discover the whereabouts of Taiwhakaea, but it had been found by a man named Māhina, who would not return it.

Poi

(Pronounced paw-ee)
Māori Entertainment

A TASK TAKEN TOO SERIOUSLY BECOMES HARD TWICE OVER.

The Poi are light balls attached to cords and are used to entertain by the swinging Poi in rythmic patterns in time to waiata [*song*].

Traditional Poi were made by stuffing dried Raupō [*bulrush*] leaves with tāhuna, the fluffy down from the Raupō seed heads or kōrino, the scraped pith from the inside of the Raupō leaf. In some areas, they were made with muka, the fibre of the Harakeke, and decorated. These days the Poi are often made with modern materials that are very effective but they are without the soft whispering sounds of the traditionally made Poi.

The origins of the Poi are not commonly known and the stories as to where they came from vary from whānau [*family*] to whānau. This is but one of those stories.

The name of the Poi comes from the "pōito," the fishing float. Pōito were used to mark the whereabouts of the tāruke [*fishing pots*] when they were lowered into the water. Tāruke were very finely woven from the Piritā [*Supplejack*] and other woods. They took many, many hours to complete and so, of course, they were matahīapo [*precious*]. Pōito were more often made from a light wood, but sometimes they were made using the raupo. Today, these pōito are much more commonly seen as a part of the wonderful Poi dance, the uri [*descendant*] of a children's game called Poipoi, which was simply swinging the Pōito.

Although born of a children's activity, it speaks of the old Māori philosophy towards work and the long or difficult task. Many a chant or song was composed while men and women worked. Māori will still laugh and joke and sing, if they can, to make the going easier and the work seem shorter.

Pūrerehua

(Pronounced poo-rare-rare-hoo-aa)
Ritual Musical Instrument

THE CALL.
TAKE CARE TO COMMUNICATE YOUR NEEDS CLEARLY.

Holding it by the stick, the Tohunga whirls "The Voice of Papatūānuku" round and round over his head. It is a low eerie humming sound and penetrates great distances through the New Zealand bush. It is a sound that is most sacred and a sound that one responds to instantly. It speaks to the Mauri of all living things, the life principle, calling to it or sending from it only what was needed.

When sickness was rife, the servants of Whiro, the bugs and the lizards, were said to be lurking. Warned by the sound of the Pūrerehua, they could be encouraged to leave. If not, called by the sound of the Pūrerehua, they could be caught and killed easily.

Rata

(Pronounced raa-taa)
Ancient Hero

RESPECT WHERE RESPECT IS DUE.

Rata was a man who lived in ancient times, long before the Māori migrated to Aotearoa. He is symbolised by te toki, the adze, for it was his task to build the Niwareka, a Waka Taua [*war canoe*]. Legend says that a great Tōtara was chosen for the waka, but Rata failed to ask the permission of the owner of the tree, Tāne Mahuta – the god of the forest. Three times he felled the tree and three times the tree was restored to the forest, as if his adze had never touched its bark. The third time, Rata hid to see how the tree was being restored. It was the birds, the creatures and the spirits of the forest who restored the tree and when their work was done, Rata confronted them. They asked him by what right had he felled the tree and demanded that he make reparation. Guided by relatives, Rata appeased the forest god and his children and the canoe was allowed to go ahead.

Raupō

(Pronounced raa-ow-paw)
Bulrush/Cattail

A GREAT TREASURE IN A SIMPLE THING. LOOK CLOSER.

Around the summer solstice in the Southern Hemisphere, the Raupō hides a golden pollen in the small flowers at the top of the bulrush. If you tap the bulrush lightly you will get a small quantity of the pollen, which can be used in cooking, giving a lovely, nutty flavour. In the old days, this pollen would be steamed in baskets to make pungapunga bread. The root of the Raupō, called Kōareare in the South Island, was also used as a food and the leaves were used for making many, many things, from poi, baskets, mats, and sandals, to thatching roofs and walls. In the South Island of New Zealand, Raupō was also used to build the Waka Mōkihi – light portable bulrush canoes.

Ruahine

(Pronounced roo-a-he-neigh)
Priestess Healer

THE WAY IS CLEAR – WHAT HOLDS YOU BACK IS NOTHING.

Tapu is a restriction of sacredness. Some things were automatically tapu by their nature, such as a new house, or the head and hair of a person, or the entire person themselves – as in the case of a Rangatira [*noble-person*] or Tohunga [*priest*]. Some things could become tapu by an action, such as the wearing of clothing by a sacred person, or the hands by the cutting of hair. A pregnant woman would be subject to tapu as she got closer to the birth of her child. Some things had tapu placed upon them for various reasons – a fishing ground when the fish became scarce, for example. The Ruahine was a Rangatira, who was firstborn in her family, and was considered by this, born with the ability to take the part of priestess in certain ceremonies, particularly the lifting of a tapu state [*Āuriuri*]. Some Ruahine were Tohunga in their own right.

Ruru

(Pronounced roo-roo)
Native Owl

THE TOHUNGA OF THE FOREST.
BE SILENT, WAIT.

The flight of the Ruru is silent. They are like ghosts in the forest until they strike upon their prey. Their stare is unmatchable, and against the Ruru, you will not win such a contest. Although the truth is that you'll never know whether or not they are staring you down, because they sleep with their eyes open. Perhaps that is true with all Tohunga!

The call of the Ruru is often feared because it is said that when the Ruru calls your name, you are about to die. However, it is not a thing to be feared, for it will not call in this way until it is your time to join your ancestors. All in its own time.

Tākeke

(Pronounced taa-qe-qe)
The Mesh of the Fishing Net

**OPPORTUNITY.
PASS IT BY AT YOUR LOSS.**

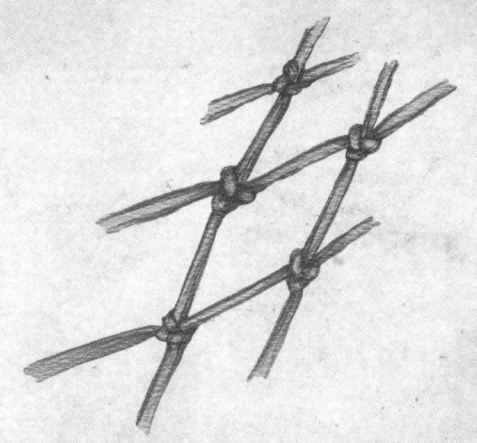

According to legend, the Māori fishing net was not of Māori origin. It was taken from the Tūrehu, the fairy people, by a man named Kahukura.

Kahukura was on a journey to another kāinga [*village*] when he came across the Tūrehu, who only came out at night to fish. The Tūrehu were a very pale people and Kahukura was very fair for a Māori man, and so he joined them in their work without being noticed. Using a trick which caused them to stop and help him repeatedly, he delayed them until dawn broke. In the light of the early morning, they saw that he was Māori and fled, leaving their nets behind.

Taniwha

(Pronounced taa-knee-far)
River Guardian

GREED. TAKE ONLY WHAT IS NECESSARY.

Taniwha is often thought to mean river monster, but it is far closer to meaning *guardian*. If one shows a river disrespect by polluting it, taking from it without reverence, or taking more than is fair, then they risk the revenge of the Taniwha living there.

Having said that much, however, the very nature of a Taniwha is often greed personified. There are many, many stories where a local Taniwha came to the end of its life at the hand of a hero because it had stolen or eaten men and women who were not its own to take.

Tarāpunga

(Pronounced taa-raa-pung-aa)
Little Red Billed Seagull

BE READY. BE ON YOUR GUARD.

When warriors attacked Mokoia Island, Rotorua, in 1823, the early morning mists were so thick that the village sentries could not see them coming. The warriors were warned by the Tarāpunga instead, who flew up in a great flock, screaming their warnings to the villagers.

Te Ao Kapurangi was a chieftainess who was present among the attackers. She had married out of her tribe, but still had relatives living at Mokoia. She had managed to negotiate the safety of her relatives on one condition. Those who "passed through her thighs" would be spared. So, calling her people to her, she stood on the top of the roof at the front of the Wharenui, which effectively made the entire house a safe haven.

A great many died that day, but because of the warnings from the Tarāpunga and the love of Te Ao Kapurangi, a great many lived, and from then on the Tarāpunga became tapu [*sacred*] to the Te Arawa people of Rotorua.

Tātarāmoa

(Pronounced taa-taa-raa-mow-aa)
Native Blackberry Vine

STRATEGY.
STOP AND RETHINK YOUR POSITION.

Tātarāmoa is also called Bush Lawyer in New Zealand and looks like an innocent straggly bush climbing up in amongst the trees. So deceptive is it, that even those who know of it can still be caught by it while walking through the New Zealand wilderness.

Removing oneself from its clutches is no easy task, as it is barbed all along every stem and every leaf. When caught within the Tātarāmoa, one cannot simply pull back without injury. You must stop and with careful patience, remove each set of barbs. This is done by moving them in the opposite direction to which you were moving, for not only are there many barbs to remove, but those that have caught you are slanting backwards, as in the teeth of the makō [*shark*] or the tuna [*eel*].

Tāwera

(Pronounced taa-where-aa)
Morning Star

ACTION.
THE TIME FOR ACTION IS NOW.

When a new building is blessed, or a ceremony is opened, it is always done with the blessing of the morning star. It has been this way for a thousand years. It is the star for active beginnings. In the old days, the appearance of Tāwera was the guiding light by which an expedition would begin, as well as a signal to attack.

Tī Kōuka

(Pronounced tee-ca-ooo-kaa)
Cabbage Tree

OUR HISTORY WILL ALWAYS BE A PART OF WHO WE ARE.

There are many reasons as to why the Tī Kōuka are special. It is known as the Cabbage Tree because the pith of its leafy heart was occasionally eaten by early settlers, who said it strongly resembled cabbage. For Māori, Tī Kōuka were an important source of food, medicine, and weaving materials. Its leaves were woven into cooking baskets when cooking in geothermal pools. Some iwi [*tribes*] would harvest and cook whole trees, baking them in great umu [*earth ovens*]. The sweet, sugary Kāuru, used to sweeten blander foods, was also made from the younger Tī Kōuka.

Some Tī Kōuka are very special. Many are remembered as altars to Atua, heroes, and wilder things – while others stand as markers to old boundaries, trails, and special places. Tī Kōuka do not grow as ordinary trees and every young tree that grows is almost always an offshoot of the matriarch tree. So it is that the Tī Kōuka will carry on long after the original tree seems to have gone.

Tī Rākau

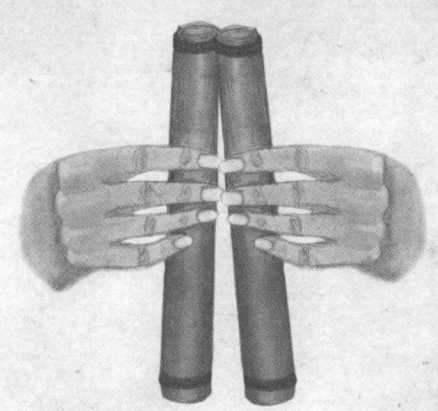

(Pronounced tee-raa-cow)
Stick Game

FOCUS ON THE TASK AT HAND.

Tī Rākau is a stick game that is often taught in New Zealand schools. Two children (sometimes four) sit opposite one another with a stick in each hand. To the tune of a popular Māori song, they will throw the Tītī [*sticks*] to each other, in certain patterns, in time to the song. Although seen these days as a children's game, Tī Rākau is a game that teaches focus, an important skill for many situations.

Tira

(Pronounced tea-raa)
Wand

CONNECTION.
THE POWER FOR CHANGE LIVES WITHIN ONESELF.

A Tira is not just a fancy stick. It was often used in matters of divination, where guidance and truth must be sought, and in rites to influence a particular outcome. It is an extension of the Tohunga that it belongs with and it has its own name. In saying that, it is also an extension of his Mana and a direct connection to his Atua. Mana is often translated as power or dominance, but these words indicate raw strength and brute force, which is incorrect. It is probably more accurate to say that Mana is a "strength of the presence" coupled with wisdom – the presence and wisdom of the Tohunga and all those who have gone before them.

Toetoe

(Pronounced toy-air-toy-air)
Native Sedge Grass

SOMETIMES THE WAY FORWARD, IS THE WAY BACK.

For the Māori, the underworld of the dead was beneath the earth, and the passage of spirits to this world was said to be through Pukakaho, the reed stalks of the Toetoe, or that of the Harakeke. When a person fell ill for no obvious reason, the illness was believed to have come about as a result of a mischievous spirit or Atua, usually because of the breaking of a tapu [*sacredness*]. The Tohunga would seek to recover the stalk through which the spirit had come and encourage the spirit back into the stalk by karakia [*prayers*].

Tōtara

(Pronounced tow-taa-raa)
Native Conifer

**THE RIGHT THING
FOR THE RIGHT PURPOSE.**

Of all the trees in the forests of Tāne, the Tōtara is one of the tallest, the strongest, and the most noble. These are some of the many reasons as to why it is called a chiefly tree, but it is especially called this because of its habit of growing deep in amongst the other trees of the forest, rather than out on the plains. The place of an Ariki [*chieftain*] is with his or her people.

As it is with Ariki, the Tōtara has special abilities as a wood, and for this reason it is the favoured tree for things that are of great importance, such as wharenui [*meeting houses*], waka [*canoes*] and whakairo [*carvings*].

Tuatara

(Pronounced too-ahh-taa-raa)
Native Lizard

HOLD DEAR THE KNOWLEDGE OF YOUR PAST, THAT YOU MAY BETTER UNDERSTAND YOUR FUTURE.

Lizards in general were often looked upon by Māori as the children of Whiro, the god of chaos and evil, and were thus kept at arms length. So much so, that they were never used as a source of food. However, the Tuatara was different, and although it was occasionally food for Ariki [*chieftains*], it was always held in great esteem. For many, the Tuatara was a kaitiaki [*guardian*] of tikanga and whakapapa [*tribal customs and histories*]. For others, its appearance of great age, at any age, was symbolic of wisdom, longevity, and perseverance. So valued was the Tuatara that some Ariki [*chieftains*] kept them as companions, and to this very day, you will see a Tuatara carved into some famous Wharenui, indicating that the Tuatara's protection remains.

Tūī

(Pronounced too-we)
Native Parson Bird

HUMILITY. EACH HAS THEIR OWN WAY.

The Tūī is called Kōkō in the South Island of New Zealand, which means a clever speaker or singer. It is especially treasured for its beautiful song, and in ancient times the Tūī was kept as a pet by distinguished families and taught to speak.

At the throat of the Tūī, you will see a flourish of white feathers – a mark of purity, for despite his beautiful song and plumage, the Tūī is not an immodest bird. He understands that to be fortunate does not make one better, and while others may not sing and talk as he does, their ways are no less important.

Tuna

(Pronounced too-nah)
Native Eel

TENACITY. WHEN ONE WAY IS NOT POSSIBLE, SEEK ANOTHER.

Of all the traditional foods, the eel has held a position of great value, even to this day. Just as Aruhe was the most dependable food from the soil, so the eel is from the waters. It is said that although the eel lives in freshwater, it is a child of Tangaroa – the god of the sea. Not truly surprising when one understands that eels are born at sea and will move through any waters to get to where they need to go, and some will even migrate over land. They are mōrehu [*survivors*] beyond measure and are well known for their tenacity and cunning. Many a hopeful eeler has sat for years trying to catch the Kuaha [*large, old eel*] of a stream or river.

Uenuku

(Pronounced oo-way-noo-koo)
The Rainbow

TAKE CARE LEST YOU LOSE THAT WHICH IS MOST DEAR TO YOU.

Uenuku was a very powerful Ariki in ancient times. He was strong, bold, and very proud. He fell in love with Hinepūkohurangi, the mist maiden. But theirs was no ordinary marriage, for Hinepūkohurangi was Porohete – of the supernatural world. Every night she came to him, but every morning, at first light, she had to leave. Uenuku wished to show his people his beautiful new wife, but she refused, warning him to say nothing until after the birth of their first child. Although Uenuku loved Hinepūkohurangi deeply, he ignored her warning and tricked her into staying by blocking up the windows of their whare [*house*]. Exposed to his people in the full light of day, she was forced to leave him forever. All his remaining days, he searched for her until he died in a land not his own. But his love for his wife did not go unrewarded, for the gods showed him favour and through them, he became the rainbow.

Waikaka

(Pronounced why-kaa-kaa)
Native Mudfish

DETERMINATION. DON'T GIVE UP, THINGS WILL COME RIGHT.

As a fish, the Waikaka has a special sense of survival, and when the streams where it lives slow to a trickle during Raumati [*summer*], it burrows into the mud and lives on the least that it can until the rains return. This is why it is called Waikaka, which means *water cunning*.

Wētā Taipo

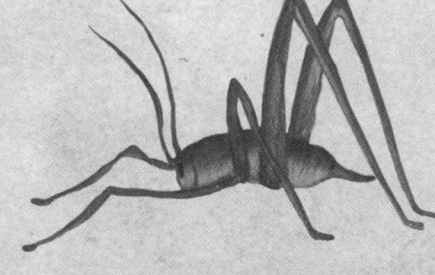

(Pronounced wet-ta-tie-paw)
Cave Weta

FEARS UNFOUNDED.

Named specifically for its ugliness, it looks dangerous and fierce, but truthfully, the Wētā is harmless. The great spike at its tail is for laying eggs. It can bite, but most likely won't. The Wētā Taipo doesn't even hunt much, preferring to scavenge off the cave floor at night. Nor will it come out on moonlit nights, for there is too much light for it to feel safe.

Ka tīmata ō te haerenga
A journey begins

Glossary

Apa
Servant

Aotearoa
New Zealand

Ariki
Chieftain or chieftainess

Atua
God or goddess

Hapū
Sub-tribe, clan, family group

Iwi
Tribe

Kāinga
Village, home

Kaitiaki
Guardian

Karakia
Prayer, salutation, incantation, or appeal to the ancestors

Kia Ora
Hello

Kupu
Words, messages

Marae
Place of gathering

Mauri
The life principle

Matakite
Seer or oracle, traditionally means the seeing of faces in dreams or visions

Māwhaiwhai
Spiderweb

Noa
Free from tapu restrictions

Pā
Fort

Puawerewere
Spider

Tangata
People

Tapu
Sacred rules of restriction

Tikanga
Customs

Tūpuna
Ancestors

Tohunga
Expert of a priestly status

Tohu
Signs, portents

Urupā
Cemetery

Waka
Canoe

Whakapapa
Family histories, genealogy

Whanau
Family

Whare
House

Wharenui
Meeting house, the house of the ancestors

Whare Vānanga
School of sacred learning

Bibliography and Recommended Reading

Auckland Museum. *Māori*. (http://www.akmuseum.org.nz, May 2004).

Beattie, Herries. *Tikao talks: Traditions and Tales Told by Teore Taare Tikao to Herries Beattie*. (Wellington, N.Z, A.H. and A.W. Reed, 1939).

Beattie, James. *Traditional Lifeways of the Southern Māori*. (Dunedin, NZ, University of Otago Press, 1994).

Cowan, James. Ngata, HM. *Legends of the Māori, Volumes 1 & 2, Mythology, Traditional History, Folklore and Poetry*. (Wellington, NZ, Harry H Tombs Limited, 1930).

Goldie, WH. MD. *Māori Medical Lore*. (New Zealand, Southern Reprints, 1998).

Hakaraia, Libby. *Matariki, The Māori New Year*. (New Zealand, Raupo Publishing [NZ] Ltd., 2008).

Hare, JB. *The Internet Sacred Texts Archive*. (http://www.sacred-texts.com/index.htm, May 2004).

Hart, Roger. Reed, AW. *Māori Myth*. (Wellington, New Zealand, A.H. & A.W. Reed Ltd., 1977).

Leather, Kay. *Māori Star Lore*. (http://www.astronomynz.org.nz/Māori, May 2004).

Māori Purposes Fund Board. *Te Ao Hou – The New World*. (New Zealand, Māori Affairs Department, 1952-1975).

Mead, Hirini Moko. *Te Toi Whakairo: The Art of Māori Carving*. (Auckland, New Zealand, Reed Publishing Ltd., 1995).

Manatū Taonga Ministry for Culture and Heritage: *Te Ara – The Encyclopedia of New Zealand*. (http://www.teara.govt.nz/en, 2012).

Ngata, HM. *English-Māori Dictionary*. (Wellington, New Zealand, Learning Media, 1993).

Puketapu-Hetet, Erenora. *Maori Weaving*. (New Zealand, Addison Wesley Longman NZ Ltd., 1999).

Riley, Murdoch. *Māori Bird Lore*. (New Zealand, Viking Sevenseas NZ Ltd., 2001).

Williams, HW. *A Dictionary of the Māori Language*. Seventh Edition. (Wellington, New Zealand, Government Printing Press, 1971).

About the Author
PA Minnell

Ko Uruaokapuarangi rātou ko Araiteuru ko Kurahaupō ko Karaerae ko Tākitimu Ngā waka tawhito
Ko Waitaha rātou ko Te Rapuwai ko Kāti Māmoe ko Ngāti Rongomaiwahine ko Ngāti Kahungunu
Ko Ngāi Tahu Ngā iwi
Ko Kāti Huirapa te hapū
Ko Arowhenua rāua ko Puketeraki ōku marae
Tihei Mauri Ora

From the ancient canoes Uruaokapuarangi, Araiteuru, Kurahaupō, Karaerae and Tākitimu.
From the tribes of Waitaha, Te Rapuwai, Kāti Māmoe, Ngāti Rongomaiwahine, Ngāti Kahungunu and Ngāi Tahu.
To the family group of Kāti Huirapa.
And Arowhenua and Puketeraki, the meeting places of my family.
It is life!

P.A. Minnell was born and raised in New Zealand and currently resides beside the sea with her husband and daughter in Wanganui, on the North Island of New Zealand.

Proud to be of New Zealand Māori and European descent, she is a dedicated Tumu Kōrero [*historian*] for her whānau [*family*]. Her whakapapa [*family history*] lines descend from chieftains, chieftainesses and tohunga, and go well back before the Great Migrations of the New Zealand Māori, in the fourteenth century. Her tribal affiliations are Kāti Māmoe and Ngāi Tahu, with kinship ties to Ngāti Kahungunu and Rongomaiwahine. Kāti Māmoe are descended from the Waitaha and the Rapuwai – two of the oldest tribes in New Zealand.

She has been an active member of the New Zealand Pagan community since 1997, and has supported many events, from public message boards to national festivals, often acting in the capacity of a key organiser and spokesperson.

As an artist, she has worked in graphic design for the last fifteen years, and in 2002, she graduated with a Bachelor of Fine Arts. Her artwork has been published in tribal publications and has featured in several local exhibitions.

PA Minnell is an avid supporter of the recovery and the revival of ethnic spirituality, both from a Pagan and a Māori perspective. She believes that the survival of these ways lies in openly sharing with anyone who is keen to learn.

"As long as we hide, scattered in the shadows,
we shall be seen as dwellers of the dark."
~Cather Steincamp, 1997